The Bee Flies In May

The Bee Flies In May

poems by

Stephen Paul Miller

MARSH HAWK PRESS ❧ NEW YORK ❧ 2002

First Edition
02 03 7 6 5 4 3 2 1

Marsh Hawk Press books are published by Poetry Mailing List, Inc.,
a not-for-profit corporation under United States
Internal Revenue Code.

Cover Drwing: Noah Miller
Author Photo: Gregory J. Holch
Cover & Book Design: Sandy McIntosh
Printed in the United States by McNaughton & Gunn
Acknowledgements appear on page 107

Library of Congress Cataloging-in-Publication Data

Miller, Stephen Paul, 1951-
The bee flies in May : poems / by Stephen Paul Miller.— 1st ed.
p. cm.
ISBN 0-9713332-3-8
1. New York (N.Y.)—Poetry. I. Title.
PS3613.I553 B44 2002
811'.54—dc21
                                    2002008144

Marsh Hawk Press
PO Box 220, Stuyvesant Station,
New York, NY 10009
www.marshhawkpress.org

to Uncle Ben, Ma, Maria, Noah, Sam, and Art

Contents

I

II

I

Poem for Noah

A buffalo looks in the mirror,
Sure he'll see himself
But a city gets in the way.
A puppy jumps out of the city.
The buffalo looks closely
And sees a silly goose
Building a nest in the mirror.
The goose overwhelms the buffalo.
He is no one but himself
And the buffalo can see it.

Sunnyside

The brown bear watches the buffalo's face,
Sees a secret in his eyes
And puts off going to work. In the secret,
She observes a storm like a holiday
And plays the golf course in his eyes.

Free Floating Holocaust

A page turns uncovering 1935.
"Mother of God!" exclaims the guinea pig.
The plastic page with pastel furnace
      flaps from Auschwitz to Birkenau,
Flaps right back, then motors into the past.

Row

I once heard Bob Dylan began writing "Desolation Row"
　　　　in the back of a cab
　　　　　　and told the cabbie to drive till it was done.
Dylan rhymes "Noah's great rainbow" with "Desolation Row"
　　　　　　and I play the song for my three-year-old son Noah.

"Is Desolation Row a small boat, Daddy?"

Concentration camp, I think,
a suburb in the Elizabethan sense:
a third world tent city outside Port-au-Prince, Lima, or
　　　　　　　　London 16 or 1700
in that it's disreputable
but the place to do business.
Send me letters from nowhere else *please*,
　　　　as Dylan says in the song, and anyway
how big is Desolation Row that you need letters?

Noah particularly likes Dylan's Mr. Jones song. After pre-
school, he bounds into our apartment screaming
"You see someone naked and say *who* is that man?!!!"

Jones tells me "I'll sue
　　if Dylan uses my first name *too*,"
then Jones tells a kapo (Jew working
　　within the vast German concentration camp
　　　　system including ghettoes and work
　　　　and transit camps)
to check the wrist brand
against the punch card
(they really only tattooed concentration camp
victims in Auschwitz and Bergen Belsen)
that initially corresponded to it.
Edwin Black's *IBM and the Holocaust*
　　　　　　(Crown, NY, 2001)
explains the human bar codes.

IBM finessed its punch card system
                              to accommodate
the advanced sorting requirements of handling
Social Security and the holocaust.

It's just that things were coming together.

Okay, Black stretches it:
Manual Nazi census taking
Might have been more efficient
Than Black would wish
And IBM didn't make the *only* punch cards, but

Still

If it were all true
              would you be surprised?
To say we're on a holocaust continuum *because that's what this poem*
              grapples with, with all its idiosyncratic connections,
              because I felt a little of my soul robbed by the 2000 election
              even if I don't know what punch card machines had to do with it,
To say we're on a holocaust continuum might confound
and insult *real* sufferers,
              I think of Tante Sonia explaining
              through almost no English
              why Stalin was worse than Hitler.
              Before Sonia does Auschwitz,
              Stalin interrupts her life by a beautiful river,
              killing her first husband, her children,
              and most of her family—
              hey my family too—a rich wonderful life
              closed to me when my nearby grandparents,
              my father's parents
              (Sonia's brother and sister-in-law),
              both die a couple of weeks apart
              when I'm three—
              in their small apartment,
              the whole family gets together
              and I feel this oddly wonderful dark expansiveness

I haven't felt since—
        even their dog Brownie died that month,

and it might be unbearably trite
        to seem to spread evil so freely around
but, as Alan Turing showed and Sonia knew,
realities converge
and no logic
is consistent.

Suburbs...holocaust...computers...
computers...holocaust...suburbs....
What am I thinking?

The ghettoes and work camps were part
        of the concentration camp system
        as secondary areas of life flowing
        into the "solution," but Emily Prager's
Eve's Tattoo (Random House, NY, 1992)
        remakes the point that the first gassings
        were directed toward the mentally ill,
        some of whose families put heat on the Nazis
        to turn that technology on the "politically
        deviant" and "'racially' marked"
and shift the emphasis from welfare reform
        to Utopian modeling. As Daniel Jonah
Goldhagen's *Hitler's Willing Executioners*
(Knopf, NY, 1996) observes,
        concentration camps were
        social experiments *too*. (It's hard for Goldhagen to
        acknowledge the aforementioned inconsistency of logic
        and convergence of things,
        since *his* logic,
        on its own terms air-tight,
        even if too air-tight,
        draws so much flack.)

Peter Novick's *The Holocaust in American Life*
        (Houghton Mifflin, Boston, 1999) says

the Holocaust has been
framed and co-opted most powerfully
by conservative Jews to justify
Israel and the uniqueness of Jewish victimhood,
quantifying suffering to no good end, and I admit
I might have been an IBM employee in a prior life.
Last spring my mother gave my son some IBM stock,
a company merely helping Hitler who was just a client
looking for "Jewish bloodlines," and that was
difficult, what with rampant assimilation and conversion.
Lots of Jews felt safe. You really couldn't tell who
        was and who wasn't. Some "Jews" hardly
                  knew themselves.
Hence, the saying they didn't know till Hitler told them.
Germany was like the U.S.—2% Jewish,
          most of them very much assimilated.
If you are Adolph Hitler and need to make good
on campaign promises, "you know you're so
ready for IBM," as the commercial goes, and
no wonder the Nazis gave IBM's CEO a gaudy medal.
By converting church conversion records and
nineteenth century Jewish community information
into punch cards, IBM and
the German government could cross-reference them
with IBM's complex 1933 census
        figures. Voila!!! I suppose
they could have done it with pencils too.
It's like the church saying they
were neutral on genocide
to save their neutrality.
"Yeah, go on."
Well, being neutral helped.
The more the church helped Nazis
       the more it helped Jews.
Who knows? Maybe. People
       can't talk to themselves
about stuff they can't admit. Fair enough.
Is this poem a concentration camp too?
Hey, a camp for concentration! Far out!!!

Who knows?
Isn't to concentrate to exclude?
Am I kapo AND Nazi?
Is my mother too?
We're victims and perpetrators.
In the early 1700's
the English garden concentrated
and marketed landscape oddity and variety.
I see a very fine, misty concentration,
a land organized for consumption.
The classic suburb bottles up nature,
according to Raymond Williams.

But where else are we supposed to go?
I think the British first used the term "concentration camp"
                            in the Boer War, but
W. S. Merwin says Americans
        in the Spanish-American War coined
        "concentration camp,"
meaning a jail for those not lucky enough
    to be soldiers or criminals
    or have an idea what is happening to them.
You concentrate a huge population
in a field or clearing, a campus, a camp.
Then (in Bill Moyer's *Power of the Word* series)
Merwin speaks of how supermarkets drain our senses.
You can't have suburbs without supermarkets.
They make you buy a ticket to Auschwitz.
They make you buy your house.
They make you self-check out at K-Mart.
Manhattan's still the best place to live
I THINK
but now to live in Manhattan
        you need to be rich enough
        to buy a huge suburban house
and then you might, like Dylan,
be so into control the street has limited appeal—
so why live in Manhattan anyway?
To walk instead of drive to K-Mart?

A missing piece is
Hernando de Soto's
Mystery of Capital
(Basic Books,
NY, 2000),

which reveals the mystery of cattle
because it tells us capital comes from
                        the late Latin for cattle.
Cattle as collateral for more cattle,
            dairy, leather, self-worth, etc.
If you've cattle you're good for everything.
How does that concern camp cattle cars and branding?
In 81 pages I'll figure it out.
I figured it out—de Soto has this notion of "dead capital"—
The Nazis called Jews "life unworthy of life"
and were intrigued with Jews as capital, dead capital.
Their uniqueness, their aura, was considered undetectable,
contagious, and all-powerful. Unconsciously,
the Nazis saw Jews as the mystery of capital
and, in the worst possible way,
wished to uncompute them,
dead end them,
treat them like cattle
that do not need to be cared for or
                        invested in, that is
        treat them like dead capital, or nearly dead cattle.

The mystery, the inside secret, of capital
is property with perfectly identifiable ownership
so that wealth can be leveraged
        and used in every which way.

Third world "suburbs,"
where I guess almost everything
                        gets made,
have wealth but are poor
since messy systems of property and ownership
stop wealth from being encoded and used.

According to de Soto,
third world nations
have great
but dead capital,
which if you think about it
makes them poorer
but more affordable
places to make stuff.

In the Nazi mind-set
no greater pleasure exists
than seeing Jews
as dead capital:
dead objects following a dead code
and working for nothing
in a minus zero world.

Historically, I think, Jews helped
          in the kind of codification
          that made capital swing
and were sometimes invited into countries
          like Poland to help
craft prosperity for others. But
the Nazis used a similar kind of codification
          to confiscate Jewish property,
much more than you'd have thought—
enough to make you think anti-Semitism
                              an excuse
but I guess Germans were anti-Semitic
                              and greedy and
crazed and sane simultaneously.
I still don't get why the Jews were most
          hated where they
          assimilated, where many wanted
          to be good Nazis too.
          Jews in Germany I think personify
          the parliamentary
          democratic government
          that gives Jews full citizenship

but seems to fail miserably.

Maybe assimilated Jews
        upset the apparently rational if obviously crazed
        zest for a "blood-based" national identity,
        says my friend Anita Feldman
        during a quick edit of this poem over dinner
        at a reasonably priced Polish restaurant on First Avenue.

        There's a guy at Brandeis who says
        Germans send Jews to western work camps
        and go after Polish shtetles
        to get Jews to make stuff
        while working with a few Poles
        as middle management
        in the eagerly anticipated new German territory
        formerly known as Poland. Okay, or

        perhaps Hitler just plain makes people feel good
        and Germans are more than happy to go along with
        his party's out of-control bureaucratic program.

                Maybe it all involves overflowing
                Nazi pleasure within the magnificent Theater
                    of Dead Capital!

Workable information manages capital.
Capital is discrete and fluid
language, law, and custom.
That's the *real* secret of capital
and why capitalism overly
        fetishizes the computer.

Punch cards sort the refrigerator
but computers find everything inside it.
You couldn't break the Nazi
Enigma code with punch card tabulation alone
and when more advanced computation
addresses the problem of storage,

storage becomes the computer's killer application,
its surprise opportunity.
Black's book doesn't mention it
but Nazi scientists develop
Random Access Memory,
which more than a decade later
greatly assists computer
storing and fetching
    (see Paul E. Ceruzzi,
The History of Modern Computing
MIT Press, 2000). Few before
the fifties could picture
the "filing cabinet" inside the computer.
A computer computed, who knew
    what a wonderful filing system
    computers could provide?
When this potential becomes apparent
and everyone in the industry
knows storage and retrieval
are where it's at,
IBM appropriates RAM
from German scientists
and RAM allows IBM
to annihilate its competitors.

Nazi era German scientists also invent magnetic tape
and by extension electronic music
and so much great sixties and seventies rock.
George Harrison said there was Hitler and then the Beatles.
They both get so much out of our system.

The more Nazis kill Jews the more
                it seems right.
Slavoj Zizek (*Looking Awry,* MIT Press, 1991)
says the holocaust is an objectless drive
that seeks to wipe out Jews
all the more the less of them there are.
Suburbs are positive commodities
obliterating inner cities.

The more people leave cities,
the more suburbs seem right,
just as Jews are negative commodities
supporting Nazi utopias

as, in a positive way,
Alan Turings's infinite laid-backness
is able to relax logic,
universalize applied mathematics,
break the German code,
and win World War II
by turning Nazi war strategy on its head,
allowing the British to get their supplies through from America
and win the Battle of Britain,
leading Hitler to attack Russia.
Thus Turing deprograms the Nazis
and invents the computer.

Alan Turing, the biggest slob perhaps ever,
                    reorders the world!

If Alan weren't gay
     he would have been even more queer!

The anti-war-leaning Turing
decoded the Nazis
"when it was thought beyond hope"
(Andrew Hodges, *Turing*, Phoenix, London, 1997)
because, Turing said, "No-one else was doing anything about
[the German code] and I could have it to myself."

          Turing was in part
          motivated by Himmler's
          order to deport even useful
          homosexual scientists
          after a conference of German scientists
          decided to stress *bold* truth.

But isn't Turing bold?

Repelling the Nazis more personally involves Turing
        than most other scientists. Turing,
expecting Germans in Britain soon,
keeps razor blades handy.

And then, after the war, British and American
                        homophobes undo Turing.

Arrested and persecuted, AlanTuring,
a Disney fan,
eats a cyanide apple,
suggesting he'll awake
when his prince comes.

Recall that Goebbels
called *Mickey Mouse* the most degenerate of art,
probably seeing in Mickey an intersection
of Jewish vermin and gay pride.

Perhaps a Silicon Valley
                incarnation of Turing
is now evoking his prince.
After Alan's high school lover,
with whom Turing does science
and wishes never to leave,
suddenly dies of TB,
Turing begins isolating the components of intelligence
to prove the death of the body does not equal death
and perhaps even locate Christopher.
Eventually, Turing posits that intelligence
                is only provable *outside* itself
when tested by a machine (or body) and its instructions.
Intelligence can use a machine;
it doesn't need a body.
Turing first needs the computer
        to solve Russell's and Hilbert's quandaries (see below)
        concerning the provability of symbolic logic—
        it was beautiful outside—
        and only, after that, to win the war.

After seeing *Snow White* on its first release
Turing often repeats the witches' incantation
that poisons the apple in their brew.

He must have associated the witches,
the Nazis, and the Cold Warriors out to get him.

When Turing dies he's working on
          curves of biological growth.

He's anxious to find non-military
          computer uses.

With Turing's loss of security clearing,
the Cold War seizes the computer.

Turing had made the proto-computer he
envisioned before the war
as an antidote for the
German Enigma machine.

That German code system changes everyday and
spits out so many permutations
decoding it with a punch card system is unthinkable.
Each operation will take too long.
The machine's guts need to be symbolic logic.
                    Forget cards.
Logic and symbols can animate faster makeshift
          operations on data through electric currents
or, at first, sonic echoes, vehicles that quickly
          yield a virtually infinite
          number of wrong answers—
precisely the Mickey Mouse answers
                    Goebbels detests, but
Turing's queer logic does not fear or dislike wrong answers.
His logic doesn't need to prove its answers.
It rather needs a base of virtually every possible answer
within the problem's range and a way to specify
which answers work. Suitability replaces provability.

Each time-consuming shuffle of physical punch cards
is a question or a search through a
              quickly generated set of lame answers.
Recall Mel Brooks saying "half the
              people in show business are gay
              and the other half Jewish.
              And it makes for a nice mix."
Similarly, a Jew comes up
              with relativity and
              a campy queer thinks of the computer—
Nazis hate relativity
              less for its Jewish roots
              than because it feels queer
              and that's the *only* reason
              we beat them to the bomb.
              They can't even imagine the *possibility*
              of Brits decoding the Enigma,
              let alone its more complex version.
              Himmler derides the British for
              letting homosexual
              scientists work. How can Mickey Mouse
              answers sink the Bismark and beat them silly?

Black is invested in the past, maybe too much so,
but *IBM and the Holocaust* is a parable of the present.
Only in a legal sense does it matter how responsible
              IBM is; it *is* responsible.
What's more important is how perhaps much more insidious
              the post-Turing Darth Vader computer
              is then the punch card machine.
It touches every facet
              of our lives in a way
              punch cards never could.
In Florida, Tennessee, and elsewhere
punch card machines
count votes poorly
while computers are increasingly used
to disenfranchise African American voters.

After the war, Turing wishes to make
    computers with a sense of wonder
and devise a math that describes
biological growth and human creativity.
(Andrew Hodges, *Alan Turing: The Enigma*,
Simon and Schuster, NY, 1983).
He expects to authenticate ESP
        by clarifying the
        spiritual connections
        sustaining everything.

They let him stop the Nazis but stop
                him—us—from reaping the rewards.

The fear the Nazis interject is too good.

In America,
there's the Depression, the Nazis/Communists,
                    and Dylan.

Do you think
Dylan was thinking one bit
about the Holocaust?
I didn't think so at first.
Maybe without the capital "H"?
It might have been like Primo Levi
saying he missed Auschwitz.
Everything after that, Levi said,
felt black and white.
My son asks me how things were
    back in the day of black and white.
The passports painted brown provided
a hint of circus color.
Is the concentration camp the circus
    Dylan says is "in town"
or do the circus and the feast
    and the carnival merely come to the Row?
How big is the Row anyway?
Dylan might not have known as that cab

cruised the city,
making a Mobius Strip that was its Row.
In the sixties, I imagine it driving
by the Electric Circus sixties style disco
and I see Astor Place as a circus,
the row between 3rd and 2nd Avenues is then
a place for feast and carnival and show.
The line his cab makes lets loose the circus space,
New York becomes a true third-world suburb,
an engine of computer, silk, and spice rows.

Similarly, Dylan's "The Gates of Eden"
 and "Desolation Row" are oddly
interchanged in my mind.
Inner and outer are weirdly charged in both.
I think this is a way to get into what concentration means.
Concentration (suburbs concentrate,
            flatten, and survey people
            in a park they have to buy into—
            Someone borrows money
            to buy lots of land
            so others can borrow
            to buy bits of it)
is about all kinds of distillation
but more than that
Dylan is jabbing from a pre-Vietnam-
            war-escalation mind-set
to the scab the sixties is built on:
the World War II Holocaust,
no, holocaust without a capital H,
so that we can proceed from the mess,
to the extent we can
and historicize the holocaust, or be in a position to,
as we now can the sixties—
I think we spent the seventies and eighties
                        and a lot of the nineties
dancing around the sixties
but when my book *The Seventies Now:*
                Culture as Surveillance,

28

(Duke University Press, Durham, 1999)
came out we faced our sixties ambivalence—
well, it had more to do with the times
seeming better and Clinton's
          relative fiscal responsibility.
Big deal, maybe,
but those were persuasive for most Americans,
which is why the Democrats won a third term
and I was able to think for a second
though I had my notions
          before Clinton—
but they did grow
while he was in office
and I can't think now,
which is why I'm working backwards
toward the holocaust,
together with so many old so-called hippies
reincarnated from the camps
who understandably saw society in a certain way.

"Somebody got lucky," says Dylan,
"BUT it was an accident."
You need a computer program
to figure out the postmodern irony.
(Oddly, Robert Venturi may have
initiated contemporary postmodernism
by emulating T. S. Eliot's modernist irony and ambiguity
as an architectural goal——It became hyper 3D irony.)
Dylan's "poetry" often trumps and qualifies itself
like computer programming
which still keeps the basic form
of Gottlob Frege's great mathematical achievement—
systematically notating mathematical sets and their qualifications.
Frege's later diaries are oddly preoccupied with questions
of what set mix makes one dangerously Jewish.
Why was his follower Ludwig Wittgenstein
really not a Jew even if he was partly or mostly Jewish?
Something's surely true of all Jews,
          Frege ruminated,

But who's the Jew?
Before this Bertrand Russell caused Frege
to stop his groundbreaking work
                              in logic
By noting that a liar can't say "I'm lying" with any reliability.
Hey Gottlob, a set can't contain itself!!!
I think the problem concerned a set not easily being
                    represented by a singular notation,
                    but Russell and Whitehead
                    really only interject
                              awkward categories of sets
                              into the dialogue.
Mathematicians later say you can bypass the problem
by going *outside*—it's such a beautiful day
(see *The Universal Computer: The Road from Leibniz to Turing*,
Martin Davis, W.W. Norton and Co., 2000)—
sort of like Dylan going in and out and in,
mixing his metaphors and screwing poetry,
the way Turing does to seamless logic,
inventing a third-world-suburb thinking machine
that can program different realities and do business *ad hoc*.

         Philosophers had long
         sought symbolic logic
         to help improve our thinking
         but Turing wanted it
         to make smart machines
         and thus describe intelligence.

Hilbert tried to qualify the "all" implicit in
 Frege's little known work.
The word "all" is just a drop in a linguistic ocean.
"All" plus A equals Set A, I think.

Godel showed you couldn't use "all" "consistently"
maybe undermining Frege and then Hilbert
but not at all bothering Turing,
who made it all good.

Even before the word "computer"
     means a machine and not a person,
Turing says it's important to
    think of computation as
    infinitely ongoing.
Think of a person computing
    on a tape—forget
    two-dimensional paper!
There *is* no other
    side—no Russell's
    Paradox scrap of paper,
    saying the answer is
    on the other side on both
    of them! The answer
    is in a here and now that stretches
            forever.
Like Dylan's words to the cabbie,
    Turing tells each operation
    to drive till it is done.
    After all, it only takes a moment
            and
    there's nowhere but this row.

Indeed, Turing shows the distinguishing feature
            of operations is to proceed *ad hoc*;
like Dylan rearranging faces
and assigning property rights
    through his floating window,
we move, Turing notes,
finally putting Frege's symbolic logic to use
by putting it to use.
Each move, Turing postulates—
I can hear him in the library cubicle next to this one—
has no natural ending
and thus requires an infinite strip of tape,
adding machine rolls
more important to Turing than teletype paper to Kerouac
and similar to Dylan in his cab.
Each move reveals an endless row

where each operation
marks one discrete and

        festive if desolate space.

Ike and Tina Tower

"They never invited me there!"
A kindergartner says
About the World Trade Center.

The only time I went up there
Was to drop something off for my father
Before express mail was everywhere.

II

The Bee Flies in May

The bee flies in May, honeying its timespace. I'm jettisoning
all the May bees before the bee drops the day
from the night on a slow buzz falling beneath it where the bee sees
the hinge
between a more convincing sap and root. I lose weight and hang
around different yet pretty flowers. When it's cold outside I
have the month of May. Maybe
I'm kidding myself.

Portrait of My Ex, Mayor Guiliani

The mayor takes me
        to a sporting event where
            he and I share
delicious adrenaline rushes skating, checking,
                    turning, and
hitting. The penguins walk all over us.

Guiliani and I discuss our addictions.
            He regards
drama as a platform to stage them.
We're talking and I'm getting comfortable.
Then he hits a painting in the mouth.
   ... I dream I'm infinitely cold, gloveless,
        locked out, my
fingertips pained as textbooks slide.
My fourth grade teacher, Mrs. Levy,
        has me carry them all home
  to brown paper wrap them.
It's colder than cold and no one's home
  and I've no key. When my lack
 of focus looks in a mirror it sees this
                  Vegas whirlpool
where my work spirals like
a nightmare of uncontrollable national debt
        come to protect me. "Hi! I'm
Mayor Guiliani, I've come to file your briefs."

Sponge

As an elephant, I gain immense pleasure being gentle and
laid back in all judicial matters.
I'm unintimidatable,
extremely phallic, and totally out there.
My nose and upper lip come
together in a hand that
sprays my head off. I have an
inlaid triangular pillow below
the ball of each foot. I guide
Stephen Paul Miller. When people jeer
at him he walks by unfazed, as do I, with my
unapproachable joy, bliss,
knowledge, and power.
Am I losing weight?
No, of course not.

Valentino

for Maria

Am I living through you?
I've seen everything w/o you.
Didn't Nilsson write "Without You"?
It's a Randy Newman song too.
On Sat., Nilsson dies,
      as if to prolong his stay in this poem
          before running to his *Times* obit.

      I want you here not Philly

    to lead me on a tour

Through Maria's world in New York,
In my peach apt., green bed.
I couldn't have found you when Bush was president.

Absolutely nothing happens when Bush is " president,"
But this *is* a Valentine that is Valentino red,
The best lovemaking maybe ever

Because it's nothing but that
But not confined to that.
Maria looks at me from an aerial view.

It's like everything is going in the opposite direction.
Time is coming toward me.
My life is in there, in Maria.

Everything floats
    or finds its spot
Maria puts everything

      in perspective.
  Objects find their

points of rest—

their homes
    where they
           rock on subsonic levels.

Cake, Book, and Candle

"Where did the baby go?"
I tell my two-year-old son that Moses grew up.
Noah turns to the beginning of the book
But sees the burning bush,
"Hot!" he screams and blows it out like a candle.
Later he points at Moses's tablets
Saying "Cake!" "Cake!" The next day I
Enter a ginger "cake" house
                  in an art gallery
            And think of Noah and Moses.

Interleague

Why don't you write poetry like
  that says Maria
as we listen to Frank Sinatra sing
"You're Just Too Marvelous for Words"
which I guess is a Meher Baba song
since he was silent
for 44 years
and marvelous
(exquisite).

Frank looks about 44 in this kinescope.
Frank looks old, Maria notes, looking at the beardy
shadows in his
face.
He's probably my age, I say.
Maria wasn't going to say that.

I dream that I am going to hug Frank good-bye.
However, my boss gives me a note
about a Chinese poetry seminar to
be
offered
where I work.
When I look up Frank is gone.

I awake with a phone in my ear and hear:
"1- We get subtler and subtler as history turns to Jell-O.
2- The millennium is a blunted instrument."

3-Next time we get married,
   says Maria, everything
   will be Sinatra.

Drop

"I felt a drop,"
Says my three-year-old son Noah.
"But it isn't raining.
Baba made a mistake!!!"

I feel a drop too
But Noah's right, it never does rain;
"Rain's not a hard word,"
Says Noah.

...The drop goes back:
"I made a mistake.
Everyone makes mistakes.
The ocean's upside down."

White pines
Slide down metal rods.
The beaver counts to 20 while
Everything in Ashoka forest hides.

Noah and the animals
Learn a cool Native American game.
A doe counts to ten and whoever
She tags becomes the new deer.

Pure Eros

This dog won't love so it stays
close, whistling in your glove.

Flies signal creamy maize elegies,
"For Eros, born on this pond's baby jetty."

Our desire
Winks at

A venerable ghost in a wispy car
Under your chewy Velveeta bridge singing:
                              "We are sub-ghosts,

Existing in non-existence, not
The other way around."

Lieberman

My eighty-something mother
Wanted Koch to succeed Reagan.

"I don't think they'd nominate a Jew," I say.

She nods. Maybe recalling something from school,
She asks, "Isn't it in the constitution?"

I don't get being Jewish because

There seems to be an inherent
        contradiction in being
        born into
A monotheism
        unless everyone
        else is.

The anti-Semites hit us over the head with that one.

My Jewish friend Eric
        says that at his girl-friend's
parents' Christmas table
        someone toasted Jesus because
        "without him we'd all be Jewish."
        But they were of Welsh/ Irish/ English descent
        so Eric and I figured
        they'd be some kind of Celtic,
Nordic, Saxon, Germanic, or Roman pagans.

        Jesus just made it easier to be Jewish!!!

Unstoned

It's time to science out.
People have had dreams
But what is identification—
It can't be good,
It hasn't spoken to me for two weeks.
We had an extremely
Expensive hotel room in Soho.

From Narrative to Landscape,
We filled the neighborhood.

We came across the bridge of landscape
To the desert, reducing the frame
To a nature reserve for lizards.
I unstoned my head.
The past rose through its patch of desert,
Strings tied to it everywhere.

Poem on Water

This is a poem moving slowly toward   My son Noah
Who told me to go to the other   bed last night so
he could   be with Mommy. You have straight light
brown   almost red hair

If it were black your hair   would look Asian but
as it is it looks quote unquote   American Pie.
It makes me feel guilty.   I should take you to
the Staten Island kid model lady   I lost that piano book
to play the Casio   With the television on you pick little
animal toys to play meticulous games.   You make me hold
a toy anteater as surrogate Winnie the Pooh
climbing a tree that's my arm. You improvise of course
but there's a certain rigidity in wanting to mimic and
repeat the character,   to regenerate it. You pee in the
potty but don't want to make the big step of
coming up for air and pooping in it.
I play with you patiently while you float toward me.

Washy

for Joy Steele and Daniel Morris

  Noah squeezes a green sponge into
the white Formica table.
Dirty greenish soap bubbles come out.
I make a mess says Noah.
He wipes the suds. "I make clean."
He squeezes some more
And the wet bubbles fall off the round table.
It's dripping he says emphatically.

Noah uses this poem to wash the table.
He eats the wash cloth, says,
"It's good" and throws it into
A corner of the dining alcove. "I want to write poem"
       he blurts and points
          to a line of my poem
            that begins
With a capital "I." Daddy draw a "T" he asks?
He scribbles near my writing and I ask him if he
                    drew a "T." "No, dinosaur," he says.

George Washington's step-grandson
                 was named Washy.
Was it Washy's daughter who married
                 Robert E. Lee?

George
      was 6'3", Martha 5 feet.
He walked when he was dying. She called
               him General.
They were cozy and lent each other their ways.
His glass of whiskey and bit of mutton
           were always ready.
Their apple pie went back to the pilgrims.

I am walking backwards through George
                    Washington's tent
Toward the history at the end of the tunnel.
You know something?
It's all forgotten.
Did you know George Washington
        made his money fishing?

        It's true. His farm was near Chesapeake Bay
        And his slaves fished with nets

And then took his name.

After his inauguration, Washington
    limps toward Broadway.

New York pops up off
    the concrete and it hits him—
Being the president's not great but good

The concrete vanishes on 77th Street.

You eat an apple as you trudge.

There's a need to stop all this:
        To pile it all in creative non-fiction.
What I'm trying to catch for George is
The big and the little infinite,
And what's this really but an office:
Like goes with like, life breaks off life,
Grab an empty cup
And this Starbucks is a discrete sea motion....

Chris says "this is about the evolution
    of America from George
Washington to Starbucks."
"Here's what's in between," I say,
    pushing the concavely

curved switch to its down
    position to drop the screen.
Sam, sitting near the VCR,
    puts in the cassette
And we see part of a new film—
        William Blake Whales
            the Crap out of an English Officer.

"My wife and I colored in my plates
As they popped out of my computer
                            like swimmers on fire,"
Blake addresses us as if he were a laid back
            high school English teacher.
He leans back in a chair behind a desk
Near the center of the front of
    a large rectangular room.
"Later my wife stays in
    the hotel with a fever
As I splash along the beach naked
    with a red sun behind me.
I dive headfirst in the sea
    but before I reach the water
A minotaur grabs my ankle and
Proverbs streak along the sand.
Hell covers the clouds.
In the court of public opinion,
    justice squats as
The judge takes notes
    while I look over his shoulder.
I become pink as a shrimp
    and revel in the grassy knoll with a starfish.
The flags unfurl down a vertical golf course.
Little sticks and twigs fly off my ass
As I surf your pyre back into my computer.

The eagle balances on my coconut.

Cross-legged, the giants huddle around me.
A rare banana pops out of the ground

          near a croquet wicket.
Held prison in a pyramid, my chest bristles.
As my wife feigns diving,
I touch her marceled hair, which is heaven.
I weep over the pink peach,
Eventually perching near a tree with human tendrils."

We leave the William Blake Theater
But our statements return for a snap edit.

George Washington has a dollar bill
 all over his fingers.
He hears something inside a tree. The buzz
                 is overwhelming.
As he says goodbye to John Lennon,
He drinks in the presidential election.

I thought this would be a long
 but construable book. However,
I find my mind is changing within it.

This is about my life folding up like an umbrella.
But where is the stick? Where is the Noah?

I drop a thousand dollars inside the telephone.

I am taking a bath with Noah. He sees me soaping
Myself and picks up another bar of soap saying
                "round and round," repeatedly soaping
                     the curve of my
forehead. Then he suddenly soaps my eyes.
As I try to find a towel, he turns the full
   liter bottle of seltzer on the floor beside
   the tub upside down, draining it on
the bathroom rug.

Noah sticks a tiny Burt figure in my mouth
And cries "No, no Daddy, go shopping, get meat!"

Later, in Noah's play "snakes eat sticks" and then
A peanut runs up to another peanut
Shouting "Wake up, Daddy!"

This poem is a wedding present. The newlyweds
    have asked that all gifts
    be donated to charity. So I'm
    giving "Washy" to my favorite one. Thank you.

Look

    daisy with a helmet on,   one hand beside its
stem   hanging from under its helmet.
I'm going to have to
jump in.   Personally I think Greenspan's
trying to maim the market
without puncturing it
to elect Bush. Okay,
       whatever.
Here's another view;   The hand is a noose and
The helmet a skull
       the upper stem a couple of
vertebrae.   Oh my God, W. Bush   it's
the Grateful Dead logo with his profile,
It's not what he always was about but the
past blends into it.
Gore is a sea horse.
I
wonder
why people don't like him.
After all, he
channels the corporate waters. Since

The mall's all eyes it's where we have to look.

Ralph Kramden Emerson Tonight

One day Ed Norton returns from Walden Pond,
Traveling by underwater pathways to Concord.
And just as Norton, a towel around his waist,
Steps from his shower,
Ralph Kramden Emerson awakes, realizing
He's dreamed the last hundred and fifty years.

(You know, like with Bobby Ewing.)

Ralph Kramden Emerson attends
A large dinner party
At Dwight Gooden's new home.
Mr. Gooden has bought a beautiful
        1830's townhouse in the 1890's.
An entertainment,
        based on an 1850's novel of manners,
        has just been staged in his drawing room.
Afterwards Dwight escorts Edith Wharton
        to a rock club of the period.
"I'm getting too old for clubs,"
    says Edith.
"You don't get old," says Dwight,
    "you just put on layers."
"Yeah, that's it," Edith responds,
    "I'm putting on another layer."
"What kind of layer?"
"You know, a more intellectual, philosophical
                        one....I have to
    write a new story tomorrow."
"Oh, that's easy," says Dwight.
"Don't say that," snaps Edith....

I am writing this
In the fish store/ sushi restaurant
On First Avenue and Fourth Street
When Allen Ginsberg walks in.
The last time I saw him

(At the Kiev),
He wrote a poem
On the spot for my magazine,
*The National Poetry Magazine
of the Lower East Side.*

I show him what I am writing now.

"I don't know who Kramden is," says Ginsberg,
"So much of the wit's lost on me."
I tell him that "Kramden" is the name of a character
Jackie Gleason played on a television show
      called *The Honeymooners*.

"I don't have a television, so I wouldn't know," Ginsberg says,
"And what's more you shouldn't trust television.
No one will know who Kramden was
In a couple of years—
Could you annotate this for me?"

Okay, Allen, in heaven listening
  to this with your mother
  in the Bronx, you're right,
  my class at St. John's University
  knew Ralph Kramden
      but they didn't know
about Bobby Ewing dreaming
      a *Dallas* season finale
      and most never heard
of the TV show at all
      and later in this poem
you'll see they never
even heard of Bernard Goetz

      But then most in my upper level
contemporary poetry class
      never heard of you— "Now that
I hear the name, I relate it to this class,"
      says my student Toni Ann

"Ginsberg's going to be mad at you," adds her friend Bill.

"Do you know Ginsberg's dead?" I ask.

"I didn't know he was alive," Bill answers.

"He died recently, didn't he?" says Linda.

"1877," I recall.

...Ralph Kramden Emerson relates a dream to Ed.
He somehow seems to be two people,
One with the middle name of "Waldo," God forbid,
And one who is fat but speedy
And somehow driving a bus in Bensonhurst.
This latter "Ralph" had dropped
The Emerson from Ralph Kramden Emerson
Upon landing a starring role
In a hit TV series of the 1950's.
In the dream, the existence of television
In the 1830's is mysteriously forgotten
So Ralph has a tremendous advantage
Over all the other seeming pioneers.
However, in 1956, at the height of Kramden's success,
Allen Ginsberg's *Howl* comes out, and,
Though it is still censored in America,
The great actor manages to smuggle a copy out of England.
"Ralph Kramden" is immeasurably moved by the work
And feels an apparently irrational urge to
Leave his hit TV show,
Travel south, and try to find his real self.
"I'm outa here," he intones and awakes to the revelation of
Ed Norton, with a towel tied around his waist,
        stepping out of the shower.
    Thank God it'd all been a dream, and it was 1837 again.

Ralph takes a Greyhound to Salem
Where he finds Nathaniel Hawthorne
Planning a history of New York.

The author is currently working on an article
In which Mayor Koch,
During his fourth inaugural address,
Breaks down and admits to
Fathering Hester Prynne's child.

Hawthorne finishes the Iran Contra scandal
And tenses as the jury comes in,
Perhaps with a verdict.
Gentlemen of the jury,
Have you reached a verdict?
No, your honor, we would like to ask Fawn Hall
A few more questions.
We have a hung jury.

In a related case,
Everyone in the courtroom
Is stunned when
Bernard Goetz is sentenced
To two years in prison on a minor
 gun possession rap.
He is inadvertently assigned
To the same cell as James Ramseur,
 one of Goetz's alleged assailants.
They get along. An important Broadway
 producer notes this
And decides to cast them
 in a revival of *The Odd Couple*
Starring Goetz as Felix
 and James Ramseur as Oscar.

The Wall Walks into the Morning

One body sticks its nose so far up another's ass it inhales
New York

Hi, my name is Walt Whitman, how much do you make?

Eli Wilentz Is Dead

What's the point of
Writing
      anything
      you can't see,
   that doesn't
    spit back at you?

Eli Wilentz, who owned the Eighth Street
      Bookshop when it was really cool,
  dies.

      Wolfman Jack follows the next day.
      It could have been me.
      He might have had a fatty
      diet.

I remember standing near the staircase
On the Eight Street Bookstore's second floor
With Dick Higgins.
Dick showed Eli *The Poetry Mailing List*—
                  a thing, a unit
Of poetry and/or art in an envelope——
And the store owner offered me a wide white pole,
Just like the one near Santa's house,
On which I could put *Poetry Mailing List* poems,
Disseminating it like a newspaper in a tiny village
In India I was once in
That could afford only one copy of the paper.

I should have kept up the project.
People were paying to subscribe.
I should have made it into something wonderful.
I'm the same bonehead everyone else is——
I wonder why everything turns out okay no matter what.
The sixties, of which *The Poetry Mailing List*
             was a 1977 part, didn't die
Anymore than the baby whom Sethe killed in *Beloved*.

We turn away but it comes back with a glow,
              like President Reagan.
Wolfman Jack was the Lucasian
Transition to Obi Wan Kenobi,
The Shaman character in *Star Wars*,
Which gave a name to the greatest defense
              industry boondoggle of our time.
Wise as he was, Wolfman
              —This Brooklyn native Robert Smith's name
Legally changed again and again—
Was greater than his wisdom.
When you die you move to the town
              in *American Graffiti*
Which is why Richard Dreyfuss
  looks so sad in the film's last shot.

2.

Eli Wilentz died again.
How do I find the data base?
I'm near the NYU Library
But have lost my reader's card.
I have to renew my alumni membership early
To check the *Times* CD ROM
And find the obituary.

3.

It was so nice on my roof this afternoon—I
              couldn't have been happier.
During a late breakfast this morning,
              my friend Anita says
Songs are a civilization's last trace.
That's certainly true about the sixties.
On the radio, Carlos Santana says that we
              come from light and go back inside,
              a reference to Jerry Garcia's death.
I only saw one Grateful Dead concert,
  and I actually went to see Bob Dylan.

The concert relaxed me, though. I walked
                    around during much of it.
It's interesting how contradictory the Dead dying is.
          I started writing this poem
This morning because I let myself do nothing
                  important or in particular on my roof.

I Deaded out, Dead space in sunshine.
The radio station is playing some nice Dead, the Dead
Controlling their overtones and oscillations well,
Making some nice figures,
Producing a dead, neutral fuzz
          like a seventies greenish gray
          Brice Marden beeswax painting.
I love fuzz. It allows for a warm, chilling drive,
Everything since 1970 got off on the wrong floor.
              The Grateful Dead figured this out early
And took their audience with them like an
Incarnation of time itself.

The group found big but out of the loop parts
                  of the record industry.
In a way, the Dead were the comprehensible front
                    end of Bob Dylan playing his
                    guitar to the wall (on Bleecker
                    Street in the early sixties).

The wall is eroding.
The floor is absorbing the speakers
And digging the marriage.

My wife Maria asks me if I can identify
                    a particular moment.
"You mean the moment," I answer, "when
          I become the cliff I hover over
    And time goes out with the tide." "Yes," she says,
                              "that's the moment."
The baby squeezes into a bottle where it writes poetry.
Mickey Mantle steps into Eli Wilentz's
          bookstore and notices this poem.

III

Dr. Shy

I want to thank the Staten
Island Pharmaceutical Society
on behalf of my mother, sister,
and brothers for the great
honor you bestow upon my
father. Although he is not here
in body we are sure he is
in spirit. We remember how
happy he was when he learned that
he was receiving this award—
he had an immense love
and respect for the pharmaceutical
profession and its variously
related functions and thought
of you, his peers, as family.

      As you well know my father
was a humble man who
honestly valued being of
service over making a profit.
In 1957, he turned an
abandoned donut shop
into a Staten Island landmark.
Unlike an international hero,
who is known for one act
or function, my father's
brand of heroism was
constant. Because he was
so kind and considerate and
trusting to everyone, in such
an unassuming and direct way,
his lifetime achievement is a
fond and guiding remembrance
to us all and his loss is
felt by so many.

"I argued with my father

about Vietnam but the man
helped build America after all."

The night before my father
had his colostomy I was
reading a detailed account
of the battle for Okinawa to him for
hours beside his hospital
bed. The marines of
World War II were one of
the few subjects that
immediately pushed my
father's interest
button—that and things like
being on the look-out for a new
drug which
he could order months
before he received a
prescription for it—
or for that matter months before
any other Staten Island
druggist, or even the
Staten Island Hospital's
pharmacy, received a
prescription for it

Because none of them
would ever order a
drug until someone
wanted it and even then
the hospital would call my
father for that drug
until enough other doctors
prescribed it.
Once I was watching
a Yankee game while
my father was sitting in his easy chair
doing paperwork
on a folding dinner stand.

When the trainer came
out to home plate my
father looked up.
                    I never saw
anyone concentrating
more intently than my
father seeing what the
trainer was putting on Graig Nettles.
A medic during the war,
my father recalled
it vividly. He
anticipated each development
and depiction in the
history I read to him.
At first he refused all sedatives
and painkillers, I
think because he was a
pharmacist he simply didn't see
any medical purpose in them.
His thinking remained
clear and lucid as his
body was shutting down
and it became hard for him to speak.
I didn't know how amazingly
bloody and gory Okinawa
was. All his life, my father
was an amazingly untalkative
                    man and
he didn't think of his past—
growing up on Staten Island,
the war, owning a drug store,
being married, having a family,
and everything else—
as anything to be talked about.
He never wanted to talk about dying,
not even with my mother.
Any mention of it would
upset him and make him turn away
or hiccup—a big symptom of colon cancer.

67

His only orientation was towards survival.
After his colostomy he came out of the
anesthesia for the operation quickly
and asked if he'd be able to
swim with his colostomy bag.
We all supposed he would.
My father couldn't see the point
or potential point in dying.
He never seemed to think about
that kind of stuff.
Talking about it wouldn't
change a thing and
he made the idea that
it would seem like some sort
of silly faddish notion.
It was as if he was in the
dead center of sanity and
the moderns and ancients
were playing with mirrors.
Of course he would have
hated this kind of family album
poem more than the least
sentimental member of you,
my audience. But still,
I feel as if I owe it to myself
to owe it to my father.
I mean God knows I have,
without exaggeration, over a hundred
other books or texts for books
in my file cabinet
typeset and everything, supposedly
for a poetry art book
with my illustrations and calligraphy
but I chose this for Lucio Pozzi's series
not because most of you don't have
wonderful fathers who care or cared
about you. Actually mine cared
about me only to the extent
that he knew me and knowing

me didn't mean descending
into unspeakable bullshit.
He didn't even know how to
give me the benefit of the doubt,
and he didn't have to, because
he didn't have to try to be nice,
he was the personification of niceness,
and he never got in my way within
his epistemological limits.
He was hard to be a kid under
because he didn't realize I
needed any more attention
than an occasional movie
after a pre-McDonald's hamburger
with all the trimmings.
He was more a soft skin than a father.
He was a sensitivity within limits which were
defined by what he loved most—
running a drug store all day
the way he wanted to run one.
He was fairly fixed in his ways
and couldn't stand anything exotic.
He was the only person I know who
didn't like the Marx Brothers.
My father wasn't like anyone else on Staten Island.
I'm not saying that because he was my father.
I never met anyone who reminded me of him and
I'm reasonably objective and always
noticing the features of other people in the
people I'm with, but
his face, features, and voice were so soft
they were hard to distinguish.
I still don't have a clear picture of him in my mind.
It's almost as if he were from another planet or
the Eastern hemisphere. Once while sitting on
the radiator beside his hospital bed
I said, "You know, I believe that
we only use our bodies." "Huh?" he said.
"You know, I believe in reincarnation."

"Makes sense," he said. I don't know how
it made sense but it didn't seem to be a
comforting idea or anything. It wasn't
worth thinking about; it just made sense.
That about half of the marines my father
landed in Okinawa with died, as
well as both the American and Japanese
commanders in chief, is only indicative
of how freakish all the hand-to-hand
deaths in the monsoon mud were. "I
had to sleep under water with my nose
sticking out," my father said. At
one point the narrator noted the officers'
great displeasure with the enlisted men
for their lack of discipline and decorum.
I asked my father if that was true.
"Everyone did their best," he said. It
bothers me that this is more about my
father than to him. But the very
impulse to make a book look like
a sixties record album sounds—with illustrations
                              and meticulous lettering
(even if you cannot see them in this form)—
is as much my father's as mine. I'm personally
and idiosyncratically producing the
written word the way my father did a
drug store. In 1975, when I was
living in Little River, South Carolina,
a friend of mine, Jim Fresino, and
I were interested in a horse running
in the Triple Crown because his name
was Avatar. (We felt as if Meher Baba
might be the avatar.) Diablo tripped up Avatar
in the Kentucky Derby so that

Foolish Pleasure won,
I remember there was a horse
        named Bombay Duck
who was hit in the head with a beer

70

can and couldn't finish.
I don't know for sure who won the Preakness
but I think it was Master Derby. But
not only did
Avatar win the Belmont
but that was the only race that Jim
and I bet on him,
through an acquaintance
who was going to India through New York.
We had told him to give away any
winnings to the Avatar
Meher Baba Trust. (My father had
sent a huge cardboard box,
the size of a trunk,
full of spare drugs and medicines
and vitamin
samples to the Meher Free
Dispensary in Ahmednagar.
Before leaving his
house for the last time
my father noticed some old clothes
that had to be thrown out.
"Does Meher Baba need any clothes?" he asked
                                    and then left.)
Since Avatar was a fourteen to one shot,
about a hundred dollars and a few weeks later
I received a pink sheet of paper in the mail from
Meher Baba's sister Mani. Above
her drawing of a little man she wrote,
"Dear Steve, Thank you for
your love donation straight from the horse's mouth.
Regards from everyone in Babatown, Mani."
I don't think Mani was thinking of me as a poet
when she wrote "straight
from the horse's mouth"
but the next time I visited India
she greeted me as "Poet" more often than "Steve."
Mani's letter was dated June 12, 1975,
the same day on which my father's

picture appeared in the *Staten Island*
Advance feeding a horse
 from the other side of a corral.
The caption read: "Alfred Miller,
President of the Staten Island Lions' Club
with horse "Poet"
at Annual Lions'
Club Horse Show." No big
coincidence, but, you know.

                              I want to thank
the Staten Island Lions'
Club on behalf of my mother, sister, and brothers
for the great honor you bestow
upon my father. Although
he is not here in body we are sure he is in spirit.
He had an immense love and respect for
                              the Lions' Club,
in its functions and what it stands
for and thought of you, his peers, as family.
That the Wednesday lunches
were perhaps the only
occasions he regularly fit into his
pharmacy schedule speaks for itself.

Horse

Rabbits have big ears to hear tiny sounds.
Noah wakes me at 5:30 and says
    "cow goes *moo*."
Animal sounds, where reality
   and yammering overlap, obsess him.
 At a nearby stable he was tickled
    to hear a real live whinny
And today at the Staten Island Children's Zoo
He was amazed by something like MEW
Coming from a cow who was just,
   according to Noah, playing with toys
And watching TV in her little zoo cell.
After hearing the charged though
 clipped mooo of a heavily smoking cow,
Noah says calmly (except for the sudden and
   terrifying cow within the statement),
        "Cow goes MOO!!!"

Noah fears and can't keep away from animals.
He puts my cap on a little brass horse head
     on the children's zoo fence
And rides the fence while holding the horse's head,
Signifying that I, Daddy, am an animal.
Zonked out on the couch, I didn't see Noah
Drawing with a green blue pen
 on the bedroom door.
As I take the pen away,
He points at an arc in his scribble——
"Nixon on a horse,"
He says with a twinkle.

73

St. Francis' Sister

I was watching the full lunar eclipse
  on Thompson St. when I heard
  a kid behind me
  compare it to Pac Man.
  His friend said "God Bless Pac Man."

The New Tompkins Square Park

I'd like to take this opportunity
to unveil to you our
plans for the New Tompkins
Square Park.
The fiberglass park benches are
being placed on the mideast quadrant
of Ninth Street, near the
Nuclear Reactor, far removed from
the faultline which runs
on a northeast diagonal from
Seventh to Eighth Streets.
It will be needed to provide
power for all the West Bank
settlers
relocating near the Seventh Street and Avenue A
corner of the park.
I think they'll prefer it
to the presently existing
basketball courts on
Avenue A and Tenth Street.
This will allow for enough
virgin land
on the southeast corner of the
park
to feed the Afghan poor
and build a
new world finance capital.
I know closing the park
for 193 years will
be tough but it's
not practical to do these
projects piecemeal. It's like
taking medicine—
you don't like it at the time but
you'll really enjoy it later.

The Gulf War Phones

SPANISH-AMERICAN WAR
Hello, Spanish-American War.

GULF WAR
Hi, is the War in Afghanistan there?

SPANISH-AMERICAN WAR
Who should I say is calling?

GULF WAR
The Gulf War.

SPANISH-AMERICAN WAR
I'm sorry, the War in Afghanistan is at a meeting right now.
He should be back in a half hour.

GULF WAR LOOKS AT HIS WATCH, CALLS BACK.

GULF WAR
Hello, this is the Gulf War. Is the War in Afghanistan
out of his meeting yet?

SPANISH-AMERICAN WAR
Hold on.

WAR IN AFGHANISTAN
War in Afghanistan speaking.

GULF WAR
Hi, uh, this is the Gulf War.
I did a performance
at your space a few years
ago. I was hoping we could
schedule an appointment
to discuss another one.

WAR IN AFGHANISTAN
Well, the way we're doing things now is,
if you send us a bio and any
reviews you might have we'll consider it.
We don't have to be held accountable.

GULF WAR
Okay, I'll be dropping something off soon.

WAR IN AFGHANISTAN
Sounds good.

Theater

I'd like to keep the concept of
   the world up there like a volleyball
Because that's how theater works,
You keep something in the air
Until time itself hangs there.
That's why the most
Innovative playwrights of the last century plus
(Ibsen, Strindberg, myself, Jarry, Beckett, Brecht, and so forth)
Have been poets—
Because conventional wisdom is wrong.
Theater, like this poem,
Has more to do with stillness than
Moving from one place to another,
It looks at the menu,
Orders "this here" demitasse and says
Bring me a cup of coffee too.

Sing Like Stephen Miller

Meaning Paul is the larynx,
     possibly. Every night
     before I go to bed I
       twist it. The night air
     Clears my throat. Then
     even the birds sing
     like Stephen Miller. Not
     just the idea
     of birds either.

Did you count every bird
     who sang just like
     me? A bird chewing
     tobacco. A bird telling
     a Canterbury Tale.
     A bird writing a love
     letter. A myopic, cussing bird.
     I am the loneliest bird
     singing like Stephen Miller.

These birds are the creation
     of language but
     one day Stephen Miller
     will be a real bird—

     the most popular bird
     singing like Stephen Miller,
     —RIGHT!

     Did you count each vote for me? One
     from Palm Beach county dancing
     in a Prince video.
     One vote wearing
     a Nicotine patch.
     A vote faxing out for Danish.
     A vote in the bush worth two hand counted votes for me.

IV

I Was on a Golf Course
the Day John Cage Died of a Stroke

As in Frank O'Hara's best known poem,
"The Day Lady Died,"
After much everyday foregrounding
A poet should perhaps discover
An "underground" celebrity's
Death through the media
But I search for little
                meaningful things,

Not exactly an appropriate tribute to John Cage.
Yesterday, the day John Cage had his
          stroke,
I saw Merce Cunningham wheeling
  his hip to hail a cab west
  on Broadway and 11th

I wonder if he was going to St. Vincent's Hospital.
Then this afternoon, about the
         time John Cage died, my friend
         Mae Fern and I were
         walking through the Staten Island Greenbelt.
         We lost our way and decided to
           find our car by hiking on a street
           alongside the nature preserve.
Mae Fern is from Arkansas and I
         asked her about the presidential election.
         She said she grew up
         in Arkansas with Bill and Hillary
         always in the background
         but as somewhat
         peripheral figures.
It was funny to leave Arkansas
         and learn more about them
On a grander scale than
         ever seemed possible at home.
Hillary had spoken to her high school and

she seemed "cold" and "mean" to her,
Yet she felt that the Clintons
        had done some good things
Such as set up the 11th grade
        exceptional students' art enhancement
Program. She said it was very "liberal"
        and cited John Cage as an example
        of the work they did. "John Cage
        was there?" I asked.
        "No, but we performed
        John Cage pieces like
        the one with about ten radios."

"Oh yeah, no one ever finds
        a radio station, right?" "Right."
I remember John Cage in 1977 in
his Bank Street basement loft,
        before he moved to the Avenue of the Americas,
        (he called the basement space "Merce's nightclub"
        and said if he ever had a view
        he'd "drink it up") typing
        a one page poem for a one
        page poetry magazine that
        Ken Deifik and I were putting out then.
He told me about a Merce Cunningham
        piece to be performed at the Minskoff Theater
        which consisted of the excess parts
        of other pieces. I said
        I'd like to see it. He gave me a ticket
        to a matinee. When I
        got there I was sitting next to him.
"Did you hear that Carter
        pardoned the draft resisters?"
        I asked.
"Oh, you mean the boys in
        Canada?" he replied.
I really wish I had shown
        him more of my poetry.
I don't think I ever sent

him my book, *Art Is Boring*
    for the Same Reason We Stayed
    in Vietnam.
I never told him that
    I didn't work as he did
    based on an urge not to repeat
    that he nourished-
I never told him I wanted to
    deprogram chance.
Once we were walking to his
    favorite West Village Xerox store
    when he asked which
    poets had most influenced me.
I told him that he had
    because he taught me
    to try to write so as not to ruin "nothing."
    "That's very hard," he said.
Once we were driving down
    34th Street when it began to
    get ominously dark.
"Sometimes one forgets
    New York is just
    a seaside town," he said.

When Listening to the Eighteen and a Half Minute Tape Gap as Electronic Music

When listening to the beginning of the eighteen
And a half minute tape gap as electronic music,
One notes a series of percussive interruptions
Of a high pitched and beautifully edged tone.
   A lulling suspension of this tone
Is punctuated by buzzes and a sudden silence
From which a very mellow static,
Composed of light, narrow, and slowly lengthening
        oscillations emerges.
The elongating of these oscillations levels
     off and then meets a thud,
A silence, and a return to the original pitch,
Which is now tinged with a more
        staticky static.

While the tape here mirthfully connotes pure electricity
       and feedback,
Other levels of the tape, and indeed of Nixon,
       seem repressed
When an underlying fuzziness oscillating
     under that tone
Takes on a thicker texture suggesting
     a fuller substance.
With an unexpected click, the purr subsides.

A narrow, airy draft is introduced and then takes over.
This is pleasant at first, as if one's ears
    were themselves the lips of waterfalls of sound
Connected to the inverse-fountain-like headphones
    with which one is required to
       listen to the Watergate tapes.
This spray, however, becomes less of an unconfrontational
    white noise and two
   pitches conflict.
These conflicting sounds end with a pinprick-like click.
The white noise again deepens.

A whir flies up like a helicopter. Its pitch loops down
                                    and up repeatedly.

A big click brings to mind
                falling off a log onto one's face,
And then the buzz intensifies. This buzz fans out,
As if to convey a sense of riding home on it.
Another click is followed by a "phttt" and a "pip"
And then a repeating round of tone rows
Of static gives the effect of sounds falling out of themselves.
These projections of sound continue and bring
            to mind a reverse and in-your face
                            kind of perspective.
This frontal quality reminds one of the tape's cloaking,
                            covering dimensions.
A tap is followed by a grinding, approaching
                plane-engine-like sound.
A powerful, lower toned buzz drops suddenly,
        as if off a table. The tone staggers.
        A piercing static fades into silence.

Today Is Red

The color of the day expands and springs through the checkerboard
Where a truck twists in the wind. It is just my way of unwinding
To bounce a ball off a piece of the Berlin wall.
Is that all I have to look forward to? I have had nothing
To say since Italy. You fluffy local, it doesn't matter what you say.
Love is following this message, which has been saved on both ends.

Poem for Agnieszka Ginko

for Katarzyna Wywial

An agreement is infinite.
You are very agreeable
But harbor conflicts
Between ceiling and roof.
We inhale seven walls
And play in the fields,
Turning the weeds into bad American presidents.

A Fictive Place Called Poland

The students in my elective class want to write
about the fictive
city where they live—Krakow. I took it as my assignment
too.
I wanted to come to Krakow
to relax but it isn't
working. There is always some little thing
like my computer being shipped
To Warsaw for a month to be fixed but not
getting fixed, or not being able
to telephone out
of the apartment for two months,
or the hot water not working, or not knowing
how to use the washing machine.
That would not be so bad but there's a certain
S and M bureaucratic attitude
going around.
There was a break-in across the hall from me
and the New Zealand woman in
the apartment there,
an English teacher who works for the university,
was told by the house manager
that it was probably one of her friends,
that nothing happened.
I am just trying to get across that my mood is often
broken. As a matter of fact, I
have lost touch with the mood that breaks.

I want to get to the country. This desire
was reinforced when Nora
(the woman from New Zealand)
introduced me to her
friend Sue and her friend Rachel,
who were going to the countryside
and would be delighted to take my wife,
baby, and me with them. But my
wife hemmed and hawed. She was afraid

of the car being too crowded

"STOP! You are revealing
all your feelings," says Agnieszka,
"You can't make American
literature from Polish history."

Sleek

Basha Willak, my 22-year-old student,
says as a child she saw
so many World War II films
the war still seemed current
and the Russian presence necessary.
Basha wants to be called Barbara
and does not miss the Russian influence
but is glad she grew up without
its American antidote.

Chris Debicki says there is a dialogue
                        in Poland
"about what people want,"
but it's on a personal level;
the burden of history, he says, is stifling
Poland and it's good to put it aside.

I wanted to write a big deal poem about Poland,
               then I gave up.
I hope you realize
you are not the right person
to write the all-encompassing poem about Poland,
one of my students, Beata, tells me.

Katarzyna Wywial speaks with a perhaps
dead Polish romanticism
when she writes, "I am a grave."
I just came back from Belorussia
and as much as the dissolution of the Soviet Union
                            still hangs over
that newly small nation, and as cataclysmic
as World War II still feels—
they do not doubt they kicked some Nazi ass.
Everyone loves the municipal victory monuments
spread throughout the city
and people even feel united
about their defeat monument

for the Belorussia war
                    dead in Afghanistan
which is a chapel built of huge weeping mothers
on the lovely Island of Tears
to which an uncontrollably
weeping angel welcomes you.
But Poland is only now (the door shuts and glows)
ending World War II.

And Poles are still embarrassed
about not existing as a political entity
for 123 years before World War I
but it wasn't their fault their borders
were so hard to defend
and they were too laid back and inherently
bitchy to emerge as a big deal military force
                    because
Poland, meaning the "land of fields,"
embodies the pastoral mind-set,
more than America does, and even in Polish cities
there's an odd sense of ease and grace and
you can still see something pre-monetary in the air.
History's on the sidelines and in a weird
way that adds to the logic
of why I didn't expect World War II
to be over over here,
and, indeed, it's still often in the news.
In America, the second World War slowly
but surely morphed into the sixties and,
in Poland, somewhere in
          me, I expected a successful sixties.

Peter, a British colleague at Jagiellonian University,
where I've been hired to teach American literature
on a Fulbright (the Fulbright somehow making me feel
as if I represent America),
tells me Poland's too touchy to talk about in Poland.
Their history has been so painful and anyway
Poles don't like to be objects of study since

for the most part only Americans do analysis.

My student Malgorzata Sokolowska says that
it is not that Polish university
 students do not know about their history—it is
that they have no way of making
                              sense of it.
So why bother?
If the clichés don't work, there is no process
in place to go beyond them,
she tells me on the last day of class and then hands
me a poem about her childhood
        memories of Russians and protests.

I'd still rather write about Poland than America.
Well, I'm not in America.
What's new in America?
If I can't deal with Polish history,
it's just that I feel somehow I'm involved in it,
that this poem's enough.

My ten-month-old son got his
hands on a transistor radio
and turned the volume dial.
Now he knows where all that noise comes from.
I want my son to play with history like that.

I hear the American economy's growing,
as is the Polish economy.
What does it mean for an economy to grow?
Unemployment's down, meaning the economy
is using what it has.
In a strong economy people make a lot of stuff
and they have the money to get that
                              stuff too.

The Polish economy is growing but
it still has to catch up to countries like Portugal.
There's lots of stuff to sell here now

and possibilities for making more stuff,
and there are people so to speak banking on it.

Its like the fifties here
in the sense that people are just now getting
their beautiful kitchens and the like.
But it's a fifties where the sixties have already happened
so there's less to look forward to,

less to put your teeth into.
My students think I would have liked it here
in the old political days before 1989.
I like it now but I wish there
was a more interesting dialogue going on.
The conversation has lost the thread the world hung on.

I am a grave that can't hold anything down.

Bohemia vanishes,
Elvis goes unsigned,
Howl is never tried,

JFK is never shot,
Vietnam escalation is not.
The American sixties is
A very sleek fifties.

Sleek 2

From a hot air balloon you can see Greenwich Village
which is actually in the hot air balloon
as it is tugged back into Yankee Stadium.

Chris Debicki says that Poland chose
capitalism for reasons of consumer
                              psychology,
that Solidarity never was about ideology.
My sense is that the Polish revolution

95

succeeded because Russia
      could not afford
         an empire, that it always was held in place
by repression—the linchpin
                of oppression
        that came undone when Solidarity
made it more difficult and costly to rule Poland.
How else was it supposed to succeed?
We only got out of Vietnam
because it was too expensive
to prop up the government.
I shocked my students last term when I asked
if the revolution might not have concerned
getting the right American brand names,
but now Anna Jankowska, at least, says,
"You were right to say last semester that
                    Mars bars
And Coca-Cola helped to overthrow the hateful system."
I think my university students are just beginning to see
pop culture as significant
            "culture."

Just as I was losing the Voice of America this morning
a Yale economist said that the world economy
was quite unusual now
because so many economic powers were maturing
together, and the United States
           had better
understand the immensities of these ten markets.
Of those he listed, I only
          remember Brazil,

India, China, Indonesia, and Poland. My student
Patrycja Krynicka says,
"Patrycja Krynicka says that
the Polish nation is anarchistic-aristocratic in its core.
It can be overwhelmed by capitalism,

thwarted by communism, but it never changes.

I'd say it is not the burden of history that changes us.
It is we who stifle history.
It is us who cannot cope with reality

and do not let history take off.
History is good for the masses.
The masses create history unaware of their role
   And there's irony in it.

Every nation has its unique spirit
just like every human being has unique nature.
Disregard what's on the surface.
Search within the soul.

Be a sculptor who sees the beautiful shapes
looking at a shapeless stone."
I love the anarchistic/aristocratic dialectic.
Is she saying that Poland
is like the Old South—politely intransigent,
even if Patrycja Krynicka says
everything is malleable in the mind of the Stoic?

Several of my students say that I expected
something impossibly exotic from
                                                    Poland.
Other of my students correct me in that
I implied that the Poles are not aware of
Polish anti-Semitism.
They tell me that everyone knows
of the violent pogrom of 1946

and other less violent de facto exilings of Jews,
                                        such as in 1968.
I crossed out the part of the poem
that they were responding to. This part:
"The Warsaw uprising was perhaps inspired by
the Jewish Warsaw ghetto uprising during
the previous summer.

"Anti-Semitism (and of course I don't speak Polish
and am just groping in the dark
more than reporting research) isn't too much brought up
because no one thinks they did very much to the Jews—
they didn't participate in the post-World War II pogroms

"or force the Jews out of town. I have heard it said that
the Jews just wanted to go to Israel—
too bad, I miss them—they were so exotic.
Too bad they'll never come back.

"Some Poles are like some blacks
in America because there is a kind of victim syndrome
at play in regard to history.
I mean blacks who ask what good it will do to talk
about slavery and race,
who think you might as well repress it.

"And I feel I should not have brought history up,
except that it seems like, you know—how the hell
can you say,
write, or teach anything if you can't bring
up unpleasant history?
That's the nub.

"This is all the more true of Poles
for whom recent history
            is no mere media circus."
Should I put that back in the poem?

Of course not. My students tell me
each Pole mourns
for some part of history
and is touchy about some other
part of history.
But what the hell,

here is another excised part of my poem—a young
Polish woman who is not in my class

but attends this university
      (the first university in Poland,
      the second oldest in Europe;
      where the Nazis first came with
      a list of professors to detain;
      alma mata of Copernicus,
      the Pope, and the poet
      who just won the Nobel Prize),
    Peter's bright student, Dorota, says:
"I'm sick of the canals
Grandpa escaped into.
You Americans don't

even begin to understand.
You don't know that we attacked
the Germans to stop the Russians, to
rule Warsaw before they rolled in.

So of course you can't blame Stalin for thoroughly
enjoying the Nazi destruction of Warsaw.
And the Russians ruled so air-tightly
that World War II lasted ten years longer than
you think—until the death of Stalin.
World War II was such a painful vacuum.
Where is there room for issues like anti-Semitism?"

That's pretty mean, though.
It doesn't take into account Poland's charm,
its valorization of domestic life.
There's something wildly tame about Poland.
Being Polish is a beautifully transparent
state that could be
a waxier melting pot than being American
if not for dark
official forces
within and without it.

My students think that I am
an interesting specimen of postmodernism

which kind of means valueless Americanism
but like a lovesick modernist
I believe in hyper interactive education—just talking—
that is Poland to me
but some of my students believe in objective
and ideal knowledge.
This ideal land is the mental fields of Poland.
American exuberance plus Polish civility
equals meta-modernism—
The powerfully compassionate music
of the seemingly unrelated.

My son came over here
         when he was four weeks old.
He got wired here.
He looks a little like R2D2. He sees
         holographs of Poland in his sleep.
I feel as if writing a poem to my son
is a good way to talk with Poland

There was an American studies conference
in Minsk last week.
I went because three of my grandparents
(your great-grandparents) are from near Minsk.
I visited the tiny village where
your grandmother's father is from.
Of course, that was a hundred years ago,

But Rudzensk is still rural, with dirt roads
and a cow pasture in the small town's
                              center
where old women with pails milk cows.
Someday I will take you there, as well
as to Sluck where Grandmom's mom is from
and a town near Vilejka, which is also about
three hours from Minsk,

where your grandfather's father was from. I didn't
have time to see the last two

            places—
Or go to a town near Poland, in the Ukraine,
Where my father's mother was born.
All my grandparents had Polish names
and came from Polish places when there was no Poland.
But of course they were Jewish non-Poles,
in the sense that Poland itself was under erasure.
But anyway I had to get back from Rudzensk to
Krakow to see you.

This is my first poem to you,
which since you do not understand
it in a top-heavy
                    sense,
is really to you a few years from now when
you are say seven—I mean I have mentioned
you before in poetry but I have never written
to the nearly seven-year-old-you.
I will read this to you now but also when you are older
and this will get more wavy with time.

So this is about the past because I have a lot
of catching up to do.
I feel myself wanting to tell
the old you about the little you,
about the time we walked in the
woods above Krakow
when you were one month old
and everyone got lost in the rain. You were
strapped to my stomach like a banjo.

I was afraid you would get hungry
but you were happy and sleepy,
even though the trail often washed away,
and I almost slipped once on the yellow trail,
which I joked went to Yellow Russia.

At that time I hardly knew
that our relatives were from White Russia,

and I had no idea what these Russian colors meant.
I did not know that no one knew.
When you were first born

you slept in a heavy stroller.
You cried regularly.
but when you came to Poland
you just slept in our bed, and you were happier.

When you were born, I sang the Merry Widow
Waltz to you and you were satisfied.
Other songs you liked were "Wonderful,
Wonderful Copenhagen,"
which I now sing COOPenhagen
and you laugh at the emphasis,
and songs from the *White Album*.
When I got back from a conference
in Washington last December
I bought you a FUTURE PRESIDENT T-shirt.

But now I am reading
you a history book called *Nixon's Piano*
that proves that every single
American president was a racist.
That's why I think you will be a politician,
 or maybe just a president,
Because you will want to figure
out how to be a non-racist president.

You are thinking about it now.
I want to go to the park and talk
it over with you.
But it is a bad May in Krakow and very cold.

You just pulled the clean laundry Mommy put on
    my lap to put away
to the floor where you are. I didn't even see you there.

Are you trying to tell me clean laundry must be used—

that political capital must be immediately played
with to end entrenched bigotry?
I think we are ready for a daring president,
"We" meaning Poland.

Right now you are lifting and waving
my shorts and laughing hysterically.
You are starting to sleep right after I bathe you.
But I have to sleep with you or you get up.
You are starting to fall backwards and laugh repeatedly.

I have to give you one or two hands to get you
up and you fall back again.
Lately, you love to put things in people's mouths.
Are you feeding me?
Do you figure that makes you as big as everyone else?

When you drew the work I used for this reading's flier,
you put the pen in my mouth before
repeatedly stabbing the paper.
Before you could draw you could write poetry.
I had a dream about sleeping in someone's house
and having a hard time getting
dressed to leave.
Was it about Poland?
Noah wants to type his answer.
        Here it is:

    gfn   fg jhhh dssssssdddzeebe7gussili
lxi9j99s.s8474 99dfst5f000do rdoood
,/.

rt5tf 5cx
nbvg

NJHKh

6b'zl lsddldx relrdll,.v,cll;lhhinbuh frt788
8y8huhib/x c t5g   vbgt ,8u.jii k   mj jkknm doooooooodot

.i

ui

Merging   representation and nation-building,
that's the end of Noah Miller's all-encompassing
poem about Poland.

Thank you
        for the time
                you have devoted to our work.

In the Air

for Hal Sirowitz

I was flying to Florida with my mother.
She looked out the window and said,
"Steve, I think we've stopped...."

A Kinkerbocker Tale

for Tom Kitts

Remember Budapest? In my heart!
I lost a pretty little bag on the subway
But now I find it in New Orleans.

That God knows no more than us
Just means she's laid back
But when she gets off her ass
We'll have big fun in the Bayou.

Acknowledgements

The author expresses appreciation to the University Seminars at Columbia University for assistance in the preparation of the manuscript for publication. The ideas presented have benefited from discussions in the University Seminar on American Studies.

Several research grants, growth grants, and merit awards from St. John's University helped make this book possible.

Some of this book's poems or their earlier versions appeared
in various journals and collections:
"Poem for Noah" and "Sunnyside" in *Le Petite Zine*; "Free Floating Holocaust" in *The New Journal*; "Portrait of My Ex, Mayor Guiliani," "The Bee Flies in May," and "A Kinkerbocker Tale," in *Poetry in Performance*; "Valentino" in *Mudfish*; "Cake, Book, and Candle," "Lieberman," and "Eli Wilentz Is Dead" in *Shofar*; "Unstoned" in *Another Chicago Magazine*; "Ralph Kramden Emerson Tonight" in *Talisman*; "Washy" in *Controlled Burn*; "The Gulf War Phones" in *Bowery Poetry Club*; "Dr. Shy" in *The Paterson Review*; "Theater" in *Scripsi*; "St. Francis's Sister" in *Appearances*; "Sing Like Stephen Miller" in the *St. Mark's Poetry Project Newsletter*; "In the Air," in *Tamarind*; "Today Is Red" and "Interleague" in *Proteus*; "I Was on a Golf Course the Day John Cage Died of a Stroke" in *Poetry New York* and *Best American Poetry 1994;* "When Listening to the Eighteen and a Half Tape Gap as Electronic Music" in *Open City;* "The New Tompkins Square Park," in *New Observations* and *The National Poetry Magazine of the Lower East Side.*

Stephen Paul Miller is a poet living in New York City with his wife Maria and their son Noah. An Associate Professor of English at St. John's University, he is the author of *The Seventies Now: Culture as Surveillance* (Duke University Press, 1999) and two books of poems, *That Man Who Ground Moths into Film* (New Observations, 1982) and *Art Is Boring for the Same Reason We Stayed in Vietnam* (Domestic, 1992), as well as co-editor with Terence Diggory of *The Scene of My Selves: New Work on New York School Poets* (the University of Maine in Orono's National Poetry Foundation, 2001). His plays have appeared at the Kitchen, P.S. 122, 8BC, the Pyramid Club, the Mudd Club, Intersection and La Mamelle in San Francisco, the University of Vermont at Burlington, and many other venues. His art work has been exhibited at P.S. 1 in Long Island City, ABC No Rio, the Ben Shawn Gallery of Paterson University, and other galleries. Among the artists with whom he has collaborated are Laurie Anderson, John Cage, Beth Anderson, Robert Ashley, Lucio Pozzi, David Shapiro, Kenward Elmslie, Taylor Mead, Kenneth Deifik, Linda Francis, Naomi Goldberg, Yvonne Jacquette, Marcia Resnick, Bruce Brand, Jim Hayes, Tom Fink, Noah Miller, Marjorie Welish, and Sandy McIntosh. A populist innovator in poetry dissemination, in the seventies Miller edited the Poetry Mailing List, which used mail art to distribute single authors such as John Cage, Kathy Acker, Joel Oppenheimer, Peter Schjeldahl, Rudy Burkhardt, David Shapiro, and many others. Around the concept of poetry readings on Saturday afternoons in Soho as art exhibitions in their own right, Miller started the Ear Inn poetry series in 1978. In 1985, Miller conceived and edited *The National Poetry Magazine of the Lower East Side,* the first "instant" magazine that authors produce on the spot. It has inspired similar magazines throughout the nation. Miller's work has appeared in *Best American Poetry 1994, Another Chicago Magazine, Open City, Shofar, New Observations, Talisman, boundary 2, St. Mark's Poetry Project Newletter, Boog City, Poetry New York, Mudfish, Le Petite Zine, Bowery Poetry Club, Scripsi, Proteus, Tamarind, Appearances, The New Journal, Poetry in Performance, the Paterson Review, Controlled Burn,* and elsewhere. Miller has received research grants from the National Endowment for the Humanities and the Gerald R. Ford Presidential Library Foundation. In 1996 and 1997, he was a Senior Fulbright Scholar in Krakow, Poland, where he was a professor at Jagiellonian University. He has also taught American literature, cultural studies, and creative writing at Columbia University, New York University, and Boricua College.